Non-Technical Summary

What are the effects of changes in government purchases of goods and services on aggregate economic activity? How are those effects transmitted? Even though such questions are central to macroeconomics and its ability to inform economic policy, there is no widespread agreement on their answer, either at the empirical or at the theoretical levels. In particular, though most macroeconomic models predict that a rise in government spending will have an expansionary effect on output, those models often differ regarding the implied effects of such a policy intervention on consumption. The standard RBC model generally predicts a decline in consumption in response to a rise in government spending, whereas the IS-LM model predicts an increase in the same variable.

What does the existing empirical evidence say regarding the consumption effects of changes in government purchases? Like several other authors that preceded us, we find that a government spending leads to a significant increase in consumption, while investment either falls or does not respond significantly. Thus, our evidence seems to be consistent with the predictions of IS-LM type models, and hard to reconcile with those of the neoclassical paradigm.

Our paper main contribution is the development of a simple dynamic general equilibrium model that can potentially account for that evidence. Our framework shares many ingredients with recent dynamic optimizing sticky price models, though we modify the latter by allowing for the presence of rule-of-thumb consumers (who do not borrow or save, consuming their wage instead), in coexistence with conventional infinite-horizon Ricardian consumers. The presence of rule-of-thumb consumers is motivated, among other considerations, by existing evidence on the failure of consumption smoothing in the face of income fluctuations or the fact that a significant fraction of households have near-zero net worth.

We show how the interaction of rule-of-thumb consumers with sticky prices and deficit financing can account for the existing evidence on the effects of government spending. Rule-of-thumb consumers insulate part of aggregate consumption from the negative wealth effects generated by the higher levels of (current and future) taxes needed to finance the fiscal expansion, while making it more sensitive to current labor income (net of current taxes). Sticky prices make it possible for real wages to increase, even if the marginal product of labor goes down, since the price markup may decline sufficiently to more than offset the latter effect. The increase in the real wage raises current labor income and hence stimulates the consumption of rule-of-thumb households. That intuition explains why both nominal rigidities and weight of rule of-thumb consumers are needed in order to obtain the desired procyclical response of consumption.

1 Introduction

What are the effects of changes in government purchases of goods and services (henceforth, government spending, for short) on aggregate economic activity? How are those effects transmitted? Even though such questions are central to macroeconomics and its ability to inform economic policy, there is no widespread agreement on their answer, either at the empirical or at the theoretical levels.

In particular, though most macroeconomic models predict that a rise in government spending will have an expansionary effect on output, those models often differ regarding the implied effects of such a policy intervention on consumption. Since the latter variable is the largest component of aggregate demand, its response is a key determinant of the size of the government spending multiplier. In that regard, the textbook IS-LM model and the standard RBC model provide a stark example of such differential qualitative predictions.

Thus, while the standard RBC model generally predicts a decline in consumption in response to a rise in government spending, the IS-LM model predicts an increase in the same variable, hence amplifying the effects of the expansion in government spending on output. Of course, the reason for the differential impact across those two models lies in how consumers are assumed to behave in each case. The RBC model features an infinitely-lived household, whose consumption decisions at any point in time are based on an intertemporal budget contraint. *Ceteris paribus*, an increase in government spending lowers the present value of after-tax income, thus generating a negative wealth effect that induces a cut in consumption.[1] In the IS-LM model consumers behave in a non-Ricardian fashion, with their consumption being

---

[1] The mechanisms underlying those effects are described in detail in Aiyagari et al. (1990), Baxter and King (1993), Christiano and Eichenbaum (1992), and Fatás and Mihov (2001), among others. In a nutshell, an increase in (non-productive) government purchases (financed by current or future lump-sum taxes) has a negative wealth effect which is reflected in lower consumption. It also induces a rise in the quantity of labor supplied at any given wage. The latter effect leads, in equilibrium, to a lower real wage, higher employment and higher output. The increase in employment leads, if sufficiently persistent, to a rise in the expected return to capital, and may trigger a rise in investment. In the latter case the size of the multiplier is greater or less than one, depending on parameter values.

a function of their current disposable income and not of their lifetime resources. Accordingly, the implied effect of an increase in government spending will depend critically on how the latter is financed, with the multiplier increasing with the extent of deficit financing.[2]

What does the existing empirical evidence say regarding the consumption effects of changes in government purchases? Can it help discriminate between the two paradigms mentioned above, on the grounds of the observed response of consumption? A number of recent empirical papers shed some light on those questions. They all apply multivariate time series methods in order to estimate the responses of consumption and a number of other variables to an exogenous increase in government spending. They differ, however, on the assumptions made in order to identify the exogenous component of that variable. In Section 2 we describe in some detail the findings from that literature that are most relevant to our purposes, and provide some additional empirical results of our own. In particular, and like several other authors that preceded us, we find that a government spending leads to a significant increase in consumption, while investment either falls or does not respond significantly. Thus, our evidence seems to be consistent with the predictions of IS-LM type models, and hard to reconcile with those of the neoclassical paradigm.

After reviewing the evidence, we turn to our paper's main contribution: the development of a simple dynamic general equilibrium model that can potentially account for that evidence. Our framework shares many ingredients with recent dynamic optimizing sticky price models,[3] though we modify the latter by allowing for the presence

---

[2]See, e.g., Blanchard (2001). The total effect on output will also depend on the investment response. Under the assumption of a constant money supply, generally maintained in textbook versions of that model, the rise in consumption is accompanied by an investment decline (resulting from a higher interest rate). If instead the central bank holds the interest rate steady in the face of the increase in government spending, the implied effect on investment is nil. However, any "intermediate" response of the central bank (i.e., one that does not imply full accommodation of the higher money demand induced by the rise in output) will also induce a fall in investment in the IS-LM model.

[3]See, e.g., Rotemberg and Woodford (1999), Clarida, Gali and Gertler (1999), or Woodford (2001).

of rule-of-thumb consumers (who do not borrow or save, consuming their wage instead), in coexistence with conventional infinite-horizon Ricardian consumers. The presence of rule-of-thumb consumers is motivated, among other considerations, by existing evidence on the failure of consumption smoothing in the face of income fluctuations (e.g., Campbell and Mankiw (1989)) or the the fact that a significant fraction of households have near-zero net worth (e.g., Wolff (1998)). On the basis of that evidence, Mankiw (2000) calls for the introduction of rule-of-thumb households in macroeconomic models, and for an examination of the policy implications of their presence.

The analysis of the properties of our model economy suggests that whether an increase in government spending raises or lowers consumption depends on the interaction of a number of factors. In particular, we show that the coexistence of sticky prices and rule-of-thumb consumers is a necessary condition for an increase in government spending to raise aggregate consumption. More interestingly, we show that for empirically plausible calibrations of the fraction of rule-of-thumb consumers, the degree of price stickiness, and the extent of deficit financing, out model predicts responses of aggregate consumption and other variables that are in line with the existing evidence.[4]

The rest of the paper is organized as follows. Section 2 describes the evidence in the literature and provides some new estimates. Section 3 lays out the model. Section 3 contains an analysis of the model's equilibrium dynamics. Section 4. examines the equilibrium response to a government spending shock under alternative calibrations, and with a special emphasis on the response of consumption and its consistency with the existing evidence. Section 5 summarizes the main findings of the paper and points to potential extensions and directions for further research.

---

[4] Ramey and Shapiro (1998) provide an alternative potential explanation of the comovements of consumption and real wages in response to a change in military spending. Their analysis is based on a two-sector model with costly capital reallocation across sectors, and in which military expenditures are concentrated in one of the two sectors (manufacturing).

2 The Evidence

In the present section we summarize the existing evidence on the responses of consumption, investment and other variables to an exogenous increase in government spending, and provide some new evidence of our own. Most of the existing evidence relies on structural vector autoregressive models, with different papers using alternative identification schemes.

Blanchard and Perotti (2002) and Fatás and Mihov (2001) identify exogenous shocks to government spending by assuming that the latter variable is predetermined relative to the other variables included in their VAR. Their most relevant findings for our purposes can be summarized as follows. First, a positive shock to government spending leads to a persistent rise in that variable. Second, the implied fiscal expansion generates a positive response in output, with the implied multiplier being greater than one in Fatás and Mihov (2001), but close to one in Blanchard and Perotti (2002). Third, in both papers the fiscal expansion leads to large (and significant) increases in consumption. Fourth, the response of investment to the spending shock is found to be insignificant in Fatás and Mihov (2001), but negative (and significant) in Blanchard and Perotti (2002). Perotti (2002) extends the methodology of Blanchard and Perotti (2002) to data for the U.K., Germany, Canada and Australia, with findings qualitatively similar to the ones obtained for the U.S. regarding the response of consumption (positive) and investment (negative) to an exogenous increase in government spending.

In related work, Mountford and Uhlig (2002) apply the agnostic identification procedure originally proposed in Uhlig (1997) (based on sign and near-zero restrictions on impulse responses) to identify and estimate the effects of a "balanced budget" and a "deficit spending" shock. As in Blanchard and Perotti (2002), Mountford and Uhlig (2002) find that government spending shocks crowd out both residential and non-residential investment, but do not reduce consumption.

Overall, we view the evidence discussed above as tending to favor the predictions of the Keynesian model, over those of the Neoclassical model (though see below for discrepant results based on alternative identification schemes). In order to assess the robustness of the above findings and the behavior of alternative variables of interest, here we provide some complementary evidence using the same identification strategy as Blanchard and Perotti (2002) and Fatás and Mihov (2001). We use quarterly U.S. data over the period 1954:I-1998:IV, drawn from the DRI database. Our baseline VAR includes government purchases (federal, state and local, GGFEQ+GGSEQ), output (GDPQ), hours (LPMHU), real interest rates -computed as the nominal rate (FYGM) minus current inflation based on the GDP deflator (GDPD)- and a fifth changing variable. For the latter we consider, in turn, consumption of nondurable and services (GCNQ+GCSQ), the real wage (LBCPU/GDPD) and non-residential investment (NRIPDC1). Moreover, in order to study the induced response of other fiscal variables we also examine the responses of (end-of-period) real public debt, taxes net of tranfers (GGFR+GGSR-GGAID-GGFTP-GGST+GGSDIV), and the (primary) budget deficit. All quantity variables are in log levels, and normalized by the size of the population of working age (P16). We included four lags of each variable in the VAR.

Figure 1 displays our main findings. Total government spending rises significantly and persistently, with a half-life of about two years. Consumption rises on impact and remains significantly above zero for more than four years. By contrast investment falls slightly and its effect dies quite rapidly.[5] Notice that under this identification the maximum effects of output and its demand components occur four to ten quarters after the shock.

The government spending multiplier on output resulting from an exogenous shock to total government spending is 0.7 at the end of the first year and 1.3 after eight quarters. Thus, our estimated multiplier effects are of a magnitude similar to the

---

[5]This result is in line with the recent cross-country evidence presented by Alesina, Ardagna and Schiantarelli (2002).

ones reported by Blanchard and Perotti (2002).[6] The sign and magnitude of these estimated VAR output responses are also consistent with the range of estimated short-run expenditure multipliers obtained using a variety of macroeconometric models.[7]

With respect to the labor variables, both hours worked and real wages appear to rise significantly during the first four quarters, following a hump-shaped pattern Moreover, and given the response of labor productivity, the rise in real wages is not enough to generate a delayed fall in the price markup, followed by a subsequent recovery into positive territory. A significant rise on real wages in response to a spending shock was also found in Fatas and Mihov (2001) when measured as compensation per hour in the non-farm business sector.

Finally, the bottom panels of Figure 1 show the response of taxes and the primary deficit. The rise in government spending causes a positive but (largely) delayed response in taxes. Accordingly, the deficit rises significantly on impact, and vanishes only after three years. Similarly, the public debt (not shown) rises slowly and starts to decrease after two years. The previous estimated responses of the fiscal variables will be used below to calibrate the fiscal policy rule in our model economy.

Qualitatively, the above results are robust to the use of military spending (instead of total government purchases) as a predetermined variable in the VAR, as in Rotemberg and Woodford (1992).

It is worth emphasizing that the findings discussed above should be interpreted as referring to the response to "regular" or ordinary changes in government spending. Other authors have focused on the economy's response to changes in fiscal policy occurring in extra-ordinary episodes, like wars or other military build-up episodes or periods of massive fiscal consolidations triggered by explosive debt dynamics.

The evidence for such episodes differs, in some dimensions, from the one based on conventional VARs presented above. This appears to be the case for the literature

---

[6]We compute the (level) multiplier as the product of the estimated elasticity (or log multiplier) with the average GDP/government spending ratio (which is roughly 5 in our sample).

[7]See Hemming, Kell and Mahfouz (2002).

that relies on the dummy variable proposed by Ramey and Shapiro (1998) to date the beginning of military build-up episodes as a measure of exogenous government spending . Using that approach, Edelberg, Eichenbaum and Fisher (1999) show that a Ramey-Shapiro episode triggers a fall in real wages, an increase in non-residential investment, and a (mild and delayed) fall in the consumption of nondurables and services, though durables consumption increases on impact. More recent work by Burnside, Eichenbaum and Fisher (2003) using a similar approach reports a flat response of aggregate consumption in the short run, followed by a small (and insignificant) rise in that variable several quarters after the Ramey-Shapiro episode is triggered.[8]

Another branch of the literature, exemplified by the work of Giavazzi and Pagano (1990), has uncovered the presence of non-Keynesian effects of large fiscal consolidations. In particular, Perotti (1999) finds evidence of a negative comovement of consumption and government spending during episodes of fiscal consolidation (and hence large spending cuts) in circumstances of "fiscal stress" (defined by unusually high debt/GDP ratios), but effects of opposite sign (and hence consistent with our evidence above) in "normal" times.

In light of that evidence, we view the model developed below as an attempt to account for the effects of government spending shocks in "normal" times (using Perotti's terminology), as opposed to extraordinary episodes. Accordingly, we explore the conditions under which a dynamic general equilibrium model with nominal rigidities and rule-of-thumb consumers can account for the positive comovement of consumption and government purchases that arises, in normal times, in response to exogenous variations in the latter variable.

---

[8] An analysis of the reasons behind the differences in the results based on the Ramey-Shapiro dummy relative to the rest of the literature lies beyond the scope of the present paper.

3 A New Keynesian Model with Rule-of-Thumb Consumers

The economy consists of two types households, a continuum of firms producing differentiated intermediate goods, a perfectly competitive final goods firm, a central bank in charge of monetary policy, and a fiscal authority. Next we describe the objectives and constraints of the different agents. Except for the presence of non-Ricardian consumers, our framework consists of a standard dynamic stochastic general equilibrium model with staggered price setting *à la Calvo*.[9]

3.1 Households

We assume a continuum of infinitely-lived households, indexed by $i \in [0,1]$. A fraction $1 - \lambda$ of households have access to capital markets where they can trade a full set of contingent securities, and buy and sell physical capital (which they accumulate and rent out to firms). We use the term (intertemporal) *optimizing* or *Ricardian* to refer to that subset of households. The remaining fraction λ of households do not own any assets or have any liabilities, and just consume their current labor income. We refer to them as *rule of thumb* or *non-Ricardian* households. Different interpretations for the latter include myopia, lack of access to capital markets, fear of saving, ignorance of intertemporal trading opportunities, etc. Campbell and Mankiw (1989) provide some aggregate evidence, based on estimates of a modified Euler equation, of the quantitative importance of such rule-of-thumb consumers in the U.S. and other industrialized economies.

---

[9] Most of the recent monetary models with nominal rigidities abstract from capital accumulation. A list of exceptions includes King and Watson (1996), Yun (1996), Dotsey (1999), Kim (2000) and Dupor (2002). In our framework, the existence of a mechanism to smooth consumption over time is critical for the distinction between Ricardian and non-Ricardian consumers to be meaningful, thus justifying the need for introducing capital accumulation explicitly.

3.1.1 Ricardian Households

Let C_t^o, and L_t^o represent consumption and leisure for optimizing/Ricardian households. Preferences are defined by the discount factor $\beta \in (0,1)$ and the period utility $U(C_t^o, L_t^o)$. A typical household of this type seeks to maximize

$$E_0 \sum_{t=0}^{\infty} \beta^t \, U(C_t^o, N_t^o) \tag{1}$$

subject to the sequence of budget constraints

$$P_t(C_t^o + I_t^o) + R_t^{-1} B_{t+1} = W_t N_t^o + R_t^k K_t^o + B_t + D_t - P_t T_t \tag{2}$$

and the capital accumulation equation

$$K_{t+1}^o = (1-\delta)\, K_t^o + \phi\left(\frac{I_t^o}{K_t^o}\right) K_t^o \tag{3}$$

At the begining of the period the consumer receives labor income $W_t N_t^o$, where W_t denotes the nominal wage, and N_t^o hours of work. He also receives income from renting his capital holdings K_t^o to firms at the (nominal) rental cost R_t^k. B_t is the quantity of nominally riskless one-period bonds carried over from period $t-1$, and paying one unit of the numéraire in period t. R_t denotes the gross nominal return on bonds purchased in period t. D_t are dividends from ownership of firms, T_t denote lump-sum taxes (or transfers, if negative) paid by these consumers. C_t^o and I_t^o denote, respectively, consumption and investment expenditures, in real terms. P_t is the price of the final good. Capital adjustment costs are introduced through the term $\phi\left(\frac{I_t^o}{K_t^o}\right) K_t^o$, which determines the change in the capital stock induced by investment spending I_t^o. We assume $\phi' > 0$, and $\phi'' \leq 0$, with $\phi'(\delta) = 1$, and $\phi(\delta) = \delta$.

In what follows we specialize the period utility to take the form:

$$U(C, L) \equiv \log C - \frac{N^{1+\varphi}}{1+\varphi}$$

where $\varphi \geq 0$.

The first order conditions for the optimizing consumer's problem can be written as:

$$1 = R_t \, E_t \, \{\Lambda_{t,t+1}\} \tag{4}$$

$$P_t Q_t = E_t \left\{ \Lambda_{t,t+1} \left[R^k_{t+1} + P_{t+1} Q_{t+1} \left((1-\delta) + \phi_{t+1} - \left(\frac{I^o_{t+1}}{K^o_{t+1}} \right) \phi'_{t+1} \right) \right] \right\} \tag{5}$$

$$Q_t = \frac{1}{\phi'\left(\frac{I^o_t}{K^o_t}\right)} \tag{6}$$

where $\Lambda_{t,t+k}$ is the stochastic discount factor for nominal payoffs given by:

$$\Lambda_{t,t+k} \equiv \beta^k \left(\frac{C^o_{t+k}}{C^o_t} \right)^{-1} \left(\frac{P_t}{P_{t+k}} \right) \tag{7}$$

and where Q_t is the (real) shadow value of capital in place, i.e., Tobin's Q. Notice that, under our assumption on ϕ, the elasticity of the investment-capital ratio with respect to Q is given by $-\frac{1}{\phi''(\delta)\delta} \equiv \eta$.

Notice that we have not listed among the first order conditions an intratemporal efficiency condition linking the consumer's marginal rate of substitution and the real wage. The reason is that, as discussed below, hours are assumed to be determined by firms (instead of being chosen by households), given the prevailing wage. Since the latter is assumed to remain above the marginal rate of substitution at all times, households find it optimal to supply as much labor as it is demanded by firms.

3.1.2 Rule-of-Thumb Households

Rule-of-thumb households do not borrow or save, possibly because of lack of access to financial markets or (continuously) binding borrowing constraints. As a results they cannot smooth their consumption path in the face of fluctuations in labor income or intertemporally substitute in response to changes in interest rates. Their period utility is given by

$$U(C_t^r, L_t^r) \tag{8}$$

and they are subject to the budget constraint:

$$P_t C_t^r = W_t N_t^r - P_t T_t \tag{9}$$

As it was the case for optimizing households, hours N_t^r are determined by firms' labor demand, and are thus not chosen optimally by each household given the wage.[10] Accordingly, the level of consumption will equate labor income net of taxes:

$$C_t^r = \frac{W_t}{P_t} N_t^r - T_t \tag{10}$$

3.1.3 The Wage Schedule

We do not model formally the details of the labor market. Instead we assume that wages are determined according to the schedule

$$\frac{W_t}{P_t} = H(C_t, N_t) \tag{11}$$

where C_t and N_t function H is increasing in both arguments, capturing both convex marginal disutility of labor and wealth effects. We interpret that function as a generalized wage schedule consistent with a variety of models of wage determination. Given the wage, each firm decides how much labor to hire, and allocates its labor demand uniformly across households, independently of their type. Accordingly, we have $N_t^r = N_t^o$ for all t.

We assume that the resulting wage markup is sufficiently high (and fluctuations sufficiently small) that the inequalities $H(C_t, N_t) > C_t^j \, N_t^\varphi$ for $j = r, o$ are assumed

---

[10]Under a perfectly competitive labor market, hours and consumption of rule-of-thumb consumers would move in opposite directions in response to movements in real wages, which we view as an implausible prediction. This is not the case under our alternative framework, which allows for the three variables to comove positively.

to be satisfied at all times. Both conditions guarantee that both type of households will be willing to meet firms' labor demand at the prevaling wage. Notice also that consistency with balanced-growth requires that H can be written as $C_t\ h(N_t)$, as we assume below.

3.1.4 Aggregation

Aggregate consumption and hours are given by a weighted average of the corresponding variables for each consumer type. Formally:

$$C_t \equiv \lambda\ C_t^r + (1-\lambda)\ C_t^o \qquad (12)$$

Similarly, aggregate investment and capital stock are given by

$$I_t \equiv (1-\lambda)\ I_t^o$$

and

$$K_t \equiv (1-\lambda)\ K_t^o$$

Finally,

$$\begin{aligned} N_t &= \lambda N_t^r + (1-\lambda)\ N_t^o \\ &= N_t^r = N_t^o \end{aligned}$$

3.2 Firms

We assume a continuum of monopolistically competitive firms producing differentiated intermediate goods. The latter are used as inputs by a (perfectly competitive) firm producing a single final good.

3.2.1 Final Goods Firm

The final good is produced by a representative, perfectly competitive firm with a constant returns technology:

$$Y_t = \left(\int_0^1 X_t(j)^{\frac{\varepsilon-1}{\varepsilon}} \, dj \right)^{\frac{\varepsilon}{\varepsilon-1}}$$

where $X_t(j)$ is the quantity of intermediate good j used as an input. Profit maximization, taking as given the final goods price P_t and the prices for the intermediate goods $P_t(j)$, all $j \in [0,1]$, yields the set of demand schedules

$$X_t(j) = \left(\frac{P_t(j)}{P_t} \right)^{-\varepsilon} Y_t$$

as well as the zero profit condition $P_t = \left(\int_0^1 P_t(j)^{1-\varepsilon} \, dj \right)^{\frac{1}{1-\varepsilon}}$.

3.2.2 Intermediate Goods Firm

The production function for a typical intermediate goods firm (say, the one producing good j) is given by:

$$Y_t(j) = K_t(j)^{\alpha} \, N_t(j)^{1-\alpha} \tag{13}$$

where $K_t(j)$ and $N_t(j)$ represents the capital and labor services hired by firm j.[11] Cost minimization, taking the wage and the rental cost of capital as given, implies the optimality condition:

$$\frac{K_t(j)}{N_t(j)} = \left(\frac{\alpha}{1-\alpha} \right) \left(\frac{W_t}{R_t^k} \right)$$

Real marginal cost is common to all firms and given by:

$$MC_t = \frac{1}{\Phi} \left(\frac{R_t^k}{P_t} \right)^{\alpha} \left(\frac{W_t}{P_t} \right)^{1-\alpha}$$

where $\Phi \equiv \alpha^{\alpha}(1-\alpha)^{1-\alpha}$.

---

[11] Without loss of generality we have normalized the level of total factor productivity to unity.

Price Setting. Intermediate firms are assumed to set nominal prices in a staggered fashion, according to the stochastic time dependent rule proposed by Calvo (1983). Each firm resets its price with probability $1-\theta$ each period, independently of the time elapsed since the last adjustment. Thus, each period a measure $1-\theta$ of producers reset their prices, while a fraction θ keep their prices unchanged.

A firm resetting its price in period t will seek to maximize

$$\max_{P_t^*} E_t \sum_{k=0}^{\infty} \theta^k \ E_t \left\{ \Lambda_{t,t+k} \ Y_{t+k}(j) \ (P_t^* - P_{t+k} \ MC_{t+k}) \right\}$$

subject to the sequence of demand constraints $Y_{t+k}(j) = X_{t+k}(j) = \left(\frac{P_t^*}{P_{t+k}}\right)^{-\varepsilon} Y_{t+k}$ and where P_t^* represents the price chosen by firms resetting prices at time t.

The first order condition for the above problem is:

$$\sum_{k=0}^{\infty} \theta^k \ E_t \left\{ \Lambda_{t,t+k} \ Y_{t+k}(j) \ \left(P_t^* - \frac{\varepsilon}{\varepsilon - 1} P_{t+k} \ MC_{t+k}\right) \right\} = 0 \qquad (14)$$

Finally, the equation describing the dynamics for the aggregate price level is given by:

$$P_t = \left[\theta \ P_{t-1}^{1-\varepsilon} + (1-\theta) \ (P_t^*)^{1-\varepsilon}\right]^{\frac{1}{1-\varepsilon}} \qquad (15)$$

3.3 Monetary Policy

In our baseline model the central bank is assumed to set the nominal interest rate $r_t \equiv R_t - 1$ every period according to a simple linear interest rate rule:

$$r_t = r + \phi_\pi \ \pi_t \qquad (16)$$

where $\phi_\pi \geq 0$ and r is the steady state nominal interest rate. An interest rate rule of the form (16) is the simplest specification in which the conditions for indeterminacy and their connection to the Taylor principle can be analyzed. Notice that it is a particular case of the celebrated Taylor rule (Taylor (1993)), corresponding to a zero coefficient on the output gap, and a zero inflation target. Rule (16) is said to satisfy the Taylor principle if and only if $\phi_\pi > 1$. As is well known, in the absence of rule-of-thumb consumers, that condition is necessary and sufficient to guarantee the uniqueness of equilibrium.[12]

3.4 Fiscal Policy

The government budget constraint is

$$P_t T_t + R_t^{-1} B_{t+1} = B_t + P_t G_t \tag{17}$$

Letting $g_t \equiv \frac{G_t - G}{Y}$, $t_t \equiv \frac{T_t - T}{Y}$, and $b_t \equiv \frac{B_t/P_{t-1} - (B/P)}{Y}$, we assume a fiscal policy rule of the form

$$t_t = \phi_b \, b_t + \phi_g \, g_t \tag{18}$$

where ϕ_b and ϕ_g are positive constants. Finally, government purchases (in deviations from steady state, and normalized by steady state GDP) evolve exogenously according to a first order autoregressive process:

$$g_t = \rho_g \, g_{t-1} + \varepsilon_t \tag{19}$$

where $0 < \rho_g < 1$, and ε_t represents an i.i.d. government spending shock with constant variance σ_ε^2.

3.5 Market Clearing

The clearing of factor and good markets requires that the following conditions are satisfied for all t :

---

[12] The "Taylor principle" refers to a property of interest rate rules for which an increase in inflation eventually leads to a more than one-for-one rise in the nominal interest rate (see Woodford (2001)).

$$N_t = \int_0^1 N_t(j)\, dj$$

$$K_t = \int_0^1 K_t(j)\, dj$$

$$Y_t(j) = X_t(j) \quad \text{for all } j$$

and

$$Y_t = C_t + I_t + G_t \tag{20}$$

3.6 Linearized Equilibrium Conditions

Next we derive the log-linear versions of the key optimality and market clearing conditions that will be used in our analysis of the model's equilibrium dynamics. Some of these conditions hold exactly, while others represent first-order approximations around a zero-inflation steady state. In general, we use lower case letters to denote the logs of the corresponding original variables, (or their log deviations from steady state).

3.6.1 Households

The log-linearized versions of the households' optimality conditions, expressed in terms of aggregate variables, are presented next.[13] Many of these optimality conditions turn out to be independent of λ, the weight of rule-of-thumb consumers in the economy.

The log-linear equations describing the dynamics of Tobin's Q and its relationship with investment are given respectively by

---
[13] See the Appendix for details.

$$q_t = \beta \; E_t\{q_{t+1}\} + [1 - \beta(1-\delta)] \; E_t\{(r^k_{t+1} - p_{t+1})\} - (r_t - E_t\{\pi_{t+1}\}) \quad (21)$$

and

$$i_t - k_t = \eta \; q_t \quad (22)$$

The log-linearized capital accumulation equation is:

$$k_{t+1} = \delta \; i_t + (1-\delta) \; k_t \quad (23)$$

The log-linearized Euler equation for optimizing households is given by

$$c^o_t = E_t\{c^o_{t+1}\} - (r_t - E_t\{\pi_{t+1}\}) \quad (24)$$

Consumption for rule-of-thumb households is given, to a first order approximation by

$$c^r_t = \left(\frac{WN}{PC^r}\right) [c_t + (1+\psi) \; n_t] - \left(\frac{Y}{C^r}\right) t_t \quad (25)$$

where $c^r_t \equiv \frac{C^r_t - C^r}{C}$, and where we have made use of the log-linearized version of wage schedule (11) consistent with balanced growth, i.e.:

$$w_t - p_t = c_t + \psi \; n_t \quad (26)$$

with ψ denoting the elasticity of wages with respect to hours, given consumption.[14]

Notice also that

$$c_t = \lambda \; c^r_t + (1-\lambda) \; c^o_t \quad (27)$$

where $c^o_t \equiv \frac{C^o_t - C^o}{C}$. This aggregate relationship, combined with the previous equation, yields the only aggregate equilibrium condition that is affected by the weight of rule-of-thumb consumers, i.e. the log-linearized aggregate Euler equation, which takes the form

---

[14] Notice that the case of pefect competition in labor markets (where real wages always equate the marginal rate of substitution) corresponds to $\psi = \varphi$.

$$c_t = E_t\{c_{t+1}\} - \frac{1}{\widetilde{\sigma}}\left(r_t - E_t\{\pi_{t+1}\} - \rho\right) - \Theta_n\, E_t\{\Delta n_{t+1}\} + \Theta_\tau\, E_t\{\Delta t_{t+1}\} \qquad (28)$$

where

$$\widetilde{\sigma} \equiv \frac{\gamma_c - \lambda(1-\alpha)\left(1-\frac{1}{\varepsilon}\right)}{\gamma_c(1-\lambda)}$$

$$\Theta_n = \frac{\lambda(1-\alpha)(1+\psi)}{\gamma_c\left(\frac{\varepsilon}{\varepsilon-1}\right) - \lambda(1-\alpha)}$$

$$\Theta_t = \frac{\lambda(1+\mu_p)}{\gamma_c\left(\frac{\varepsilon}{\varepsilon-1}\right) - \lambda(1-\alpha)}$$

with $\gamma_c = \frac{C}{Y}$ being the share of consumption on output (which, as shown in the Appendix, does not depend on λ). Notice that $\lim_{\lambda \to 0} \widetilde{\sigma} = 1$, $\lim_{\lambda \to 0} \Theta_n = 0$, and $\lim_{\lambda \to 0} \Theta_\tau = 0$.

Two features of the above derivations are worth stressing. First, Euler equation (28) is the only log-linear equilibrium condition involving aggregate variables which depends on λ. More precisely, the presence of rule-of-thumb households influences the equilibrium dynamics through its effects on the coefficient on expected employment growth in the aggregate Euler equation. Second, even under non-distorsionary taxation schemes, the presence of rule-of-thumb consumers imply that the consumption equation depends upon taxes.

3.6.2 Firms

Log-linearization of (14) and (15) around the zero inflation steady state yields the familiar equation describing the dynamics of inflation as a function of the deviations of the average (log) markup from its steady state level

$$\pi_t = \beta\, E_t\{\pi_{t+1}\} - \lambda_p\, \mu_t^p \qquad (29)$$

where $\lambda_p = \frac{(1-\beta\theta)(1-\theta)}{\theta}$ and ignoring constant terms,

$$\mu_t^p = (y_t - n_t) - (w_t - p_t) \qquad (30)$$

or, equivalently,

$$\mu_t^p = (y_t - k_t) - (r_t^k - p_t) \qquad (31)$$

Furthermore, it can be shown that the following aggregate production function holds, up to a first order approximation:

$$y_t = (1-\alpha)n_t + \alpha k_t \qquad (32)$$

3.6.3 Market clearing

Log-linearization of the market clearing condition of the final good around the steady state yields:

$$y_t = \gamma_c \, c_t + \gamma_i \, i_t + g_t \qquad (33)$$

where $\gamma_i \equiv \frac{I}{Y}$ represents the share of investment on output in the steady state.

3.6.4 Fiscal Policy

Linearization of the government budget constraint (17) around a steady state with zero debt and a balanced primary budget yields

$$b_{t+1} = (1+\rho)(b_t + g_t - t_t)$$

where $\rho \equiv \beta^{-1} - 1$ pins down the steady state interest rate. Plugging in the fiscal policy rule assumed above we obtain:

$$b_{t+1} = (1+\rho)(1-\phi_b) b_t + (1+\rho)(1-\phi_g) g_t \qquad (34)$$

Hence, under our assumptions, a necessary and sufficient condition for non-explosive debt dynamics is given by

$$\phi_b > \frac{\rho}{1+\rho}$$

4 Analysis of Equilibrium Dynamics

Combining all the equilibrium conditions involving aggregate variables and doing some straightforward though tedious substitutions we can obtain a system of stochastic difference equations describing the log-linearized equilibrium dynamics of our model economy of the form

$$\mathbf{A} \, E_t\{\mathbf{x}_{t+1}\} = \mathbf{B}\mathbf{x}_t + \varepsilon_t \tag{35}$$

where $\mathbf{x}_t \equiv (n_t, c_t, \pi_t, k_t, b_t, g_{t-1})'$. The elements of matrices $\mathbf{A}$ and $\mathbf{B}$ are all functions of the underlying structural parameters, as shown in the Appendix. The present section is devoted to the analysis of the determinacy of the model's equilibrium dynamics. We start by describing the calibration that we use as a benchmark.

Each period is assumed to correspond to a quarter. With regard to preference parameters, we set the discount factor β equal to 0.99. The elasticity of substitution across intermediate goods, ε, is set to 6, a value consistent with a steady state markup μ^p of 20 percent. The rate of depreciation δ is set to 0.025. Following King and Watson (1996), η (the elasticity of investment with respect to q) is equal to 1.0. The elasticity of output with respect to capital, α, is assumed to be $\frac{1}{3}$, a value roughly consistent with income share given the assumed low steady state price markup. All the previous parameters are kept at their baseline values throughout the present section. Next we turn to the parameters for which we conduct some sensitivity analysis, distinguishing between the non-policy and the policy parameters.

Our baseline setting for the weight of rule-of-thumb households λ is $\frac{1}{2}$. This is within the the range of estimated values in the literature of the weight of the rule-of-thumb behavior (see Mankiw (2000)). The fraction of firms that keep their prices unchanged, θ, is given a baseline value of 0.75, which corresponds to an average price duration of one year. We set our baseline value for the elasticity of wages with respect to hours (ψ) to be equal to 0.2. This is consistent with Rotemberg and

Woodford's (1997, 1999) calibration of the elasticity of wages with respect to output of 0.3 combined with an elasticity of output with respect to hours of $\frac{2}{3}$.

Finally, the policy parameters are chosen as follows. We set the size of the response of the monetary authority to inflation, ϕ_π, to 1.5, a value commonly used in empirical Taylor rules (and one that satisfies the so-called Taylor principle). For the two parameters describing the fiscal rule (18) we use the information provided by our VAR analysis. In particular, we computed a historical decomposition of governtment spending, taxes and debt due to the identified government spending shock. Then, we use the exogenous variations due to these shocks in the variables to regress that of taxes on government spending and debt. The corresponding estimated value for ϕ_g was 0.12 with standard error, 0.06; while the parameter for the response of taxes to debt, ϕ_b, was 0.30 with standard error 0.06. The estimated value for ϕ_g is in line with the evidence reported by Blanchard and Perotti (2002), while the estimated parameter for ϕ_b is slightly higher than the (unconditional) estimate of Bohn (1998).

The steady state balanced primary budget is set to an average government spending share (s_g) of 0.2 and ρ_g, the autoregressive coefficient in the government spending process, is 0.9. These two latter values are also consistent with the U.S. evidence, including the impulse response of government spending to its own shock shown in Figure 1.

Much of the sensitivity analysis below focuses on the share of rule-of-thumb households (λ) and its interaction with parameters θ, η, ψ and ϕ_π. Given the importance of the fiscal rule parameters in the determination of aggregate consumption (and, indirectly, of other variables) we will also analyze the effect of alternative values for the policy parameters ϕ_b, ϕ_g, and ρ_g.

4.1 Rule-of-Thumb Consumers, Indeterminacy, and the Taylor Principle

Next we provide an analysis of the conditions that guarantee the uniqueness of equilibrium. A more detailed analysis of those conditions for an economy similar to the one considered here (though without a government sector) can be found in Galí, López-Salido and Vallés (2003). There we show that the presence of rule-of-thumb consumers can alter dramatically the equilibrium properties of an otherwise standard dynamic sticky price economy. In particular, under certain parameter configurations the economy's equilibrium may be indeterminate (and thus may display stationary *sunspot* fluctuations) even when the interest rate rule is one that satisfies the Taylor principle (which corresponds to $\phi_\pi > 1$ in our model).

Figure 2 illustrates that phenomenon for the model developed in the previous section under the baseline calibration. In particular the figure displays the region in the parameter space (λ, θ) associated with a unique equilibrium and multiple equilibrium, in a neighborhood of the steady state. We see that indeterminacy arises whenever a high degree of price stickiness coexists with a sufficiently large weight of rule-of-thumb households. Both frictions are thus seen to be necessary in order for indeterminacy to emerge as a property of the equilibrium dynamics. As discussed by Galí, López-Salido and Vallés (2003), that finding holds irrespective of the assumed values for the real wage elasticity ψ although the size of the uniqueness region shrinks as ψ increase. The figure also makes clear that the equilibrium is unique under our baseline calibration ($\lambda = \frac{1}{2}$, $\theta = 0.75$).

5 The Effects of Government Spending Shocks

In the present section we analyze the effects of shocks to government spending in the model economy described above. In particular, we focus on the conditions under which an exogenous increase in government spending has a positive effect on consumption, as found in much of the existing evidence. Throughout we restrict ourselves to calibrations for which the equilibrium is unique.

Figure 3 shows the contemporaneous response of output, consumption and investment (all normalized by steady state output) to a positive government spending shock, as a function of the autoregressive coefficient in the government spending process, ρ_g. The remaining parameters are kept at their baseline values. The figure shows clearly the possibility of crowding-in of consumption, i.e., an increase in consumption in response to a rise in government spending. That crowding-in effect (and the consequent enhancement of the multiplier) is decreasing in ρ_g, since higher values of that parameter are associated with stronger (negative) wealth effects lowering consumption of Ricardian households. Yet, we that even for values of ρ_g higher than 0.9 a positive (though relatively small) effect on aggregate consumption emerges. Notice also that the response of investment to the same shock is negative over the whole admissible range of ρ_g although with values very close to unity (i.e., near-random walk processes for government spending) that response becomes nill.

Figure 4 summarizes the impact multiplier under some alternative calibrations. Each calibration assumes a limiting value for one (or two) parameters, while keeping the rest at their baseline values. Thus, the *flexible price* scenario assumes $\theta = 0$, the *no rule-of-thumb* economy assumes $\lambda = 0$, the *neoclassical* calibration combines both flexible prices and lack of rule-of-thumb consumers ($\theta = \lambda = 0$). Notice that when prices are fully flexible, or when all consumers are optimizing (or when both features coexist, as under the neoclassical calibration) consumption is always crowded-out in response to a rise in government spending, independently of the degree of persistence of the latter. This illustrates the difficulty of reconciling the evidence with standard dynamic general equilibrium models.

To complete the picture, Figure 5 displays the dynamic responses of output, its three demand components, hours and real wages to a positive government spending shock under the baseline calibration, and compares them to those generate by a neoclassical economy ($\theta = \lambda = 0$). Not surprisingly, the adjustment of the three demand components and the output is monotonic, implying that the sign of the conditional correlations can already be inferred from the impact responses shown above. Futhermore, in the baseline model, and in contrast with the neoclassical model, the increase in aggregate hours coexists with an increase in real wages. At the end of the Figure we also display the response of taxes and deficit. Notice that the patern of both variables is close to the one estimated in the data (Figure 1)

The graphs in Figure 6 summarize the sensitivity of the impact multipliers to variations in four structural parameters λ, θ, η and ψ to a one percent government spending shock. In the upper left panel we observe that the impact response of consumption and output are increasing in the share of rule-of-thumb consumers (λ), whereas the response of investment is decreasing in the same parameter. Interestingly, values of lambda higher than 0.3 lead to an increase in consumption, while investment is slightly negative. In the upper right panel the degree of price stickiness is indexed by parameter θ. A key result seems to emerge: the size of the response of output and its two components (consumption and investment), is increasing in the degree of price rigidities. Again, values of θ slightly higher than 0.6 are consistent with a positive response of aggregate consumption to an ingrease in govenrent spending. The two lower panels show the impact multipliers when the degree of capital adjustment costs, η, and the real wage elasticity, ψ change. High capital adjustment costs (i.e., low η) tend to damp investment fluctuations, but enhance the response of consumption and output. Finally, we notice the impact multipliers are not very sensitive to changes in the elasticity of real wages with respect to hours (i.e. ψ), provided that the rest of the parameters are at their baseline values.

Figure 7 displays a similar set of graphs showing the impact response of output, consumption and investment as a function of the three policy parameters (ϕ_π, ϕ_g, ϕ_b). Qualitatively, the top panel appears as the mirror image to the one shown in Figure 6 with the degree of price stickiness: the stronger the central bank's response to inflation (ϕ_π), the weaker is the impact of a government spending shock on output and its components. That finding may not be surprising since in staggered price setting models of the sort analyzed here, the central bank can approximate arbitrarily well the flexible price equilibrium allocation by following an interest rate rule that responds with sufficient strength to inflation. The middle and bottom panels in Figure 7 show the sensibility of the multiplier effects to changes in the two fiscal rule parameters. A clear result emerges from these figures. A positive comovement of consumption and government spending requires a sufficiently high response of taxes to debt (high ϕ_b) and a sufficiently low response of taxes to current government spending (i.e., low ϕ_g) (and thus a larger increase in the budget deficit on impact).

6 Summary and Assessment of the Model

In the previous analysis we have shown how the interaction between the fraction of rule-of-thumb households (whose consumption equals their labor income) and sticky prices (modeled as in the recent New Keynesian literature) makes it possible to generate an increase in consumption in response to a persistent expansion in government spending, in a way consistent with much of the recent evidence. Rule-of-thumb consumers insulate part of aggregate consumption from the negative wealth effects generated by the higher levels of (current and future) taxes needed to finance the fiscal expansion, while making it more sensitive to current labor income (net of current taxes). Sticky prices make it possible for real wages to increase, even if the marginal product of labor goes down, since the price markup may decline sufficiently to more than offset the latter effect. The increase in the real wage raises current labor income and hence stimulates the consumption of rule-of-thumb households. That intuition explains why both nominal rigidities and weight of rule-of-thumb consumers are needed in order to obtain the desired procyclical response of consumption. Most importantly, that result can be obtained with configurations of parameter values which are consistent with the exiting evidence and/or which conventionally assumed in the business cycle literature. Thus, we view our results as providing a potential solution to the seeming conflict between empirical evidence and the predictions of existing DSGE models regarding the efects of government spending shocks.

Our theoretical analysis assumes that the increase in government spending is financed by means of lump-sum taxes (current or future). If only distortionary labor and/or capital income taxes were available to the government, the response of the different macroeconomic variables to a government spending shock will generally differ from the one that obtains in the economy with lump-sum taxes analyzed above, and will depend on the composition and timing of the taxation. We leave the analysis of that case for future research.

Appendix

Steady State Analysis

The market clearing condition for final goods implies:

$$\begin{aligned}
\gamma_c &= 1 - \frac{I}{Y} - \frac{G}{Y} \\
&= 1 - \frac{\delta\alpha}{\alpha\left(\frac{Y}{K}\right)} - \gamma_g \\
&= (1 - \gamma_g) - \frac{\delta\alpha}{(\rho+\delta)(1+\mu^p)}
\end{aligned}$$

where the last equality follows from the fact that in the steady state $\frac{R^k}{P} = \frac{\alpha}{1+\mu^p}\frac{Y}{K}$ (implied by the constant marginal cost) and $\frac{R^k}{P} = (\rho+\delta)$ (implied by a constant Q). Notice that this share of consumption on total output it is independent of the share of rule-of-thumb consumers.

Derivation of the Reduced Dynamical System

The equilibrium conditions describing the model dynamics are given by expressions (26)-(34). Now we reduce those conditions to the five variable system (35) in terms of hours, consumption, inflation, capital and government spending.

The first equation in the system (35) corresponds to the linearized capital accumulation equation (23), with i_t substituted out using market clearing condition (33) and replacing y_t subsequently using the production function (32):

$$k_{t+1} = \left(1 - \delta + \frac{\delta\alpha}{1-\widetilde{\gamma}_c}\right)k_t + \frac{\delta(1-\alpha)}{1-\widetilde{\gamma}_c}n_t - \frac{\delta\,\gamma_c}{1-\widetilde{\gamma}_c}c_t - \frac{\delta}{1-\widetilde{\gamma}_c}g_t \qquad (36)$$

where $\widetilde{\gamma}_c = \gamma_c + \gamma_g$. In order to derive the second equation in (35) we start by rewriting the inflation equation (29) in terms of variables contained in $\mathbf{x}_t$. Using (30) and (26) we obtain an expression for the marginal cost as a function of the consumption output ratio and aggregate hours

$$\mu_t = y_t - c_t - (1+\psi)n_t \qquad (37)$$

Substituting the previous expression (37) into (29), and making use of (32) yields the second equation in (35)

$$\begin{aligned}\pi_t &= \beta\ E_t\{\pi_{t+1}\} + \lambda_p\ [c_t - y_t + (1+\psi)\ n_t] \\ &= \beta\ E_t\{\pi_{t+1}\} + \lambda_p\ c_t - \alpha\lambda_p\ k_t + (\alpha+\psi)\lambda_p\ n_t\end{aligned} \qquad (38)$$

To obtain the aggregate consumption Euler equation we substitute expression (25) into expression (27) which yields

$$\begin{aligned}c_t &= \lambda\left(\frac{WN}{PC}\right)[c_t + (1+\psi)\ n_t] - \lambda\left(\frac{Y}{C}\right) t_t + (1-\lambda)\ c_t^o \\ &= \lambda\left(\frac{WN}{PC}\right)[c_t + (1+\psi)\ n_t] - \lambda\left(\frac{Y}{C}\right) t_t + (1-\lambda)\ c_t^o \\ &= \frac{\lambda\ (1+\psi)(1-\alpha)}{\gamma_c\ (1+\mu^p) - \lambda\ (1-\alpha)}\ n_t - \frac{\lambda\ (1+\mu^p)}{\gamma_c\ (1+\mu^p) - \lambda\ (1-\alpha)}\ t_t + \frac{\gamma_c\ (1+\mu^p)(1-\lambda)}{\gamma_c\ (1+\mu^p) - \lambda\ (1-\alpha)}\ c_t^o\end{aligned}$$

We can use the previous equation to substitute for c_t^o in (24) to obtain an Euler-like equation for aggregate consumption:

$$\begin{aligned}c_t &= E_t\{c_{t+1}\} - \frac{\gamma_c\ (1+\mu^p)(1-\lambda)}{\gamma_c\ (1+\mu^p) - \lambda\ (1-\alpha)}\ (r_t - E_t\{\pi_{t+1}\}) \\ &\quad - \frac{\lambda\ (1+\psi)\ (1-\alpha)}{\gamma_c\ (1+\mu^p) - \lambda\ (1-\alpha)}\ E_t\{\Delta n_{t+1}\} \\ &\quad + \frac{\lambda\ (1+\mu^p)}{\gamma_c\ (1+\mu^p) - \lambda\ (1-\alpha)}\ E_t\{\Delta t_{t+1}\}\end{aligned}$$

or, more compactly,

$$c_t = E_t\{c_{t+1}\} - \frac{1}{\widetilde{\sigma}}\ (r_t - E_t\{\pi_{t+1}\}) - \Theta_n\ E_t\{\Delta n_{t+1}\} + \Theta_t\ E_t\{\Delta t_{t+1}\}$$

where $\widetilde{\sigma} = \left(\frac{\gamma_c(1+\mu^p) - \lambda(1-\alpha)}{\gamma_c(1-\lambda)(1+\mu^p)}\right)$, $\Theta_n = \frac{\lambda(1-\alpha)(1+\psi)}{\gamma_c(1+\mu^p) - \lambda(1-\alpha)}$ and $\Theta_t = \frac{\lambda\ (1+\mu^p)}{\gamma_c(1+\mu^p) - \lambda(1-\alpha)}$, which are the coefficients of expression (28) in the text.

Plugging into the previous Euler equation the interest rate rule (16), the fiscal rule (18), and using the fact the the government spending follows a first order autoregressive process (19) we obtain the third equation in (35):

$$c_t - \Theta_n\, n_t + \frac{\phi_\pi}{\widetilde{\sigma}}\pi_t = E_t\{c_{t+1}\} + \frac{1}{\widetilde{\sigma}} E_t\{\pi_{t+1}\} - \Theta_n\, E_t\{n_{t+1}\} \qquad (39)$$
$$+\Theta_t \phi_b\, \Delta b_{t+1} + \Theta_t \phi_g (\rho_g - 1)\, g_t$$

In order to derive the fourth equation we first combine (37) and (31) to obtain $r_t^k - p_t = c_t - k_t + (1+\psi)n_t$. The latter expression and the interest rate rule (16), allows us to rewrite the equations describing the dynamics of Tobin's q and investment as follows:

$$i_t - k_t = \beta\, E_t\{(i_{t+1} - k_{t+1})\}$$
$$+\eta[1 - \beta(1-\delta)]\, [E_t\{c_{t+1}\} - k_{t+1} + (1+\psi)\, E_t\{n_{t+1}\}]$$
$$-\eta\phi_\pi\, \pi_t + \eta\, E_t\{\pi_{t+1}\}$$

Finally, substituting the relationship

$$i_t - k_t = \left(\frac{1}{1-\widetilde{\gamma}_c}\right)[(1-\alpha)n_t - \gamma_c c_t - g_t - (1 - \widetilde{\gamma}_c - \alpha)k_t]$$

(which can be derived by combining the goods market clearing condition with the production function) into the previous equation and rearranging terms we obtain the fourth equation of our dynamical system

$$(1-\alpha)\, n_t - \gamma_c\, c_t - (1 - \widetilde{\gamma}_c - \alpha)\, k_t + (1-\widetilde{\gamma}_c)\eta\phi_\pi\, \pi_t = [\omega(1+\psi) + \beta(1-\alpha)]\, E_t\{n_{t+1}\}$$
$$+(\omega - \beta\gamma_c)\, E_t\{c_{t+1}\}$$
$$-[\omega + \beta(1 - \widetilde{\gamma}_c - \alpha)]\, k_{t+1}$$
$$+(1-\widetilde{\gamma}_c)\eta\, E_t\{\pi_{t+1}\} \qquad (40)$$
$$+(1-\beta\rho_g)\, g_t$$

where $\omega \equiv \eta[1 - \beta(1-\delta)](1-\widetilde{\gamma}_c) > 0$.

The last two equations of the system correspond to expression (34) describing the debt accumulation and the autoregressive process for government spending (19).

Hence the system of equations (36), (38), (39), (40), (34), and (19) can be written in a matrix form as follows

$$\mathbf{A}\, E_t\{\mathbf{x}_{t+1}\} = \mathbf{B}\, \mathbf{x}_t + \varepsilon_t$$

where $\mathbf{x}_t \equiv [n_t,\, c_t,\, \pi_t,\, k_t,\, b_t,\, g_{t-1}]'$, and

$$\mathbf{A} \equiv \begin{bmatrix} 0 & 0 & 0 & 1 & 0 & \frac{\delta}{1-\tilde{\gamma}_c} \\ 0 & 0 & \beta & 0 & 0 & 0 \\ -\Theta_n & 1 & \frac{1}{\sigma} & 0 & \Theta_t\phi_b & \Theta_t(\rho_g - 1)\phi_g \\ \omega(1+\psi)+\beta(1-\alpha) & \omega-\beta\gamma_c & (1-\tilde{\gamma}_c)\eta & -[\omega+\beta(1-\tilde{\gamma}_c-\alpha)] & 0 & (1-\beta\rho_g) \\ 0 & 0 & 0 & 0 & 1 & -(1+\rho)(1-\phi_g) \\ 0 & 0 & 0 & 0 & 0 & 1 \end{bmatrix}$$

$$\mathbf{B} \equiv \begin{bmatrix} \frac{\delta(1-\alpha)}{1-\tilde{\gamma}_c} & -\frac{\delta\,\gamma_c}{1-\tilde{\gamma}_c} & 0 & 1-\delta+\frac{\delta\alpha}{1-\tilde{\gamma}_c} & 0 & 0 \\ -(\alpha+\psi)\lambda_p & -\lambda_p & 1 & \alpha\lambda_p & 0 & 0 \\ -\Theta_n & 1 & \frac{\phi_\pi}{\sigma} & 0 & \Theta_t\phi_b & 0 \\ 1-\alpha & -\gamma_c & (1-\tilde{\gamma}_c)\eta\phi_\pi & \tilde{\gamma}_c+\alpha-1 & 0 & 0 \\ 0 & 0 & 0 & 0 & (1+\rho)(1-\phi_b) & 0 \\ 0 & 0 & 0 & 0 & 0 & \rho_g \end{bmatrix}$$

References

AIYAGARI, R., L.CHRISTIANO AND M. EICHENBAUM (1990): "Output, Employment and Interest Rate Effects of Government Consumption", *Journal of Monetary Economics*, 30, 73-86.

ALESINA, A, S. ARDAGNA, R. PEROTTI AND F. SCHIANTARELLI (2002): "Fiscal Policy, Profits, and Investment," *American Economic Review,* 92 (3), 571-589.

BAXTER, M. AND R. KING (1993): "Fiscal Policy in General Equilibrium", *American Economic Review*, 83, 315-334.

CAMPBELL, J. Y. AND N. GREGORY MANKIW (1989): "Consumption, Income, and Interest Rates: Reinterpreting the Time Series Evidence," in O.J. Blanchard and S. Fischer (eds.), *NBER Macroeconomics Annual 1989*, 185-216, MIT Press.

CHRISTIANO, L. AND M. EICHENBAUM (1992): " Current Real Business Cycles Theories and Aggregate Labor Market Fluctuations", *American Economic Review*, 82, 430-450.

BLANCHARD, O. (2001): *Macroeconomics,* Prentice Hall.

BLANCHARD, O. AND R. PEROTTI (2002): "An Empirical Characterization of the Dynamic Effects of Changes in Government Spending and Taxes on Output," *Quarterly Journal of Economics,117, 4, 1329-1368.*

BOHN, H. (1998): "The Behavior of Public Debt and Deficits", *The Quarterly Journal of Economics* 113(3), 949-964.

BURNSIDE, C., M. EICHENBAUM AND J. FISHER (2003): "Fiscal Shocks and their Consequences", NBER WP nº 9772.

CAMPBELL, J. Y. AND N. G. MANKIW (1989): "Consumption, Income, and Interest Rates: Reinterpreting the Time Series Evidence," in O.J. Blanchard and S. Fischer (eds.), *NBER Macroeconomics Annual 1989*, 185-216, MIT Press.

CALVO, G. (1983): "Staggered Prices in a Utility Maximizing Framework", *Journal of Monetary Economics*, 12, 383-398.

CLARIDA, R., J. GALÍ AND M. GERTLER (1999): " The Science of Monetary Policy: A New Keynesian Perspective", *Journal of Economic Literature*, 37, 1661-1707.

DOTSEY, M. (1999): "Structure from Shocks," Federal Reserve Bank of Richmond, Working Paper n° 99-6.

DUPOR, B. (2002): "Interest Rate Policy and Investment with Adjustment Costs," mimeo.

EDELBERG, W., M. EICHENBAUM, AND J. FISHER (1999), "Understanding the Effects of Shocks to Government Purchases," *Review of Economic Dynamics*, 2, 166-206.

FATÁS, A. AND I. MIHOV (2001): "The Effects of Fiscal Policy on Consumption and Employment: Theory and Evidence," INSEAD, mimeo.

GALÍ, J., J. D. LÓPEZ-SALIDO AND J. VALLÉS (2003): "Rule-of- Thumb Consumers and the Design of Interest Rate Rules", Working Paper 0320, Banco de España.

GIAVAZZI, F., AND M. PAGANO (1990): "Can Severe Fiscal Contractions be Expansionary? Tales of Two Small European Countries" in O.J. Blanchard and S. Fischer (eds.), *NBER Macroeconomics Annual 1990*, MIT Press.

HEMMING, R., M. KELL AND S. MAHFOUZ (2002): " The effectiveness of Fiscal Policy in Stimulating Economic Activity-A Review of the Literature, IMF WP n⁰ 02/208.

KIM, J. (2000): "Constructing and estimating a realistic optimizing model of monetary policy," *Journal of Monetary Economics*, 45, 2, 329-359.

KING, R., AND M. WATSON (1996): "Money, Prices, Interest Rates and the Business Cycle" *Review of Economics and Statistics*, 78, 35-53.

MANKIW, N. G. (2000): "The Savers-Spenders Theory of Fiscal Policy," *American Economic Review*, 90, 2, 120-125.

MOUNTFORD, A. AND H. UHLIG (2000): "What are the Effects of Fiscal Policy Shocks?, Discussion Paper 31, Tilburg University, Center for Economic Research.

PEROTTI, R. (1999): "Fiscal Policy in Good Times and Bad," *Quarterly Journal of Economics*, 114, 4, 1399-1436.

RAMEY, V. AND M. SHAPIRO (1998): "Costly Capital Reallocation and the Effect of Government Spending," *Carnegie-Rochester Conference Series on Public Policy*, 48, 145-194.

ROTEMBERG, J. AND M. WOODFORD (1992): "Oligopolistic Pricing and the Effects of Aggregate Demand on Economic Activity", *Journal of Political Economy*, 100, 1153-1297.

ROTEMBERG, J. AND M. WOODFORD (1997): "An Optimization Econometric Framework for the Evaluation of Monetary Policy" in O.J. Blanchard and S. Fischer (eds.), *NBER Macroeconomics Annual 1997*, MIT Press.

— (1999):"Interest Rate Rules in an Estimated Sticky Price Model" in J.B. Taylor (ed.), *Monetary Policy Rules*, University of Chicago Press and NBER.

TAYLOR, J. B. (1993): "Discretion versus Policy Rules in Practice," *Carnegie Rochester Conference Series on Public Policy*, December 1993, 39, 195-214.

WOLFF, E. (1998): "Recent Trends in the Size Distribution of Household Wealth", *Journal of Economic Perspectives* 12, 131-150.

WOODFORD, M. (2001): "The Taylor Rule and Optimal Monetary Policy," *American Economic Review* Vol. 91, n°. 2, 232-237.

YUN, T. (1996): "Nominal Price Rigidity, Money Supply Endogeneity, and Business Cycles," *Journal of Monetary Economics* 37, 345-370.

Figure 1. Responses to a Government Spending Shock

Sample Period: 1954:1-1998:4

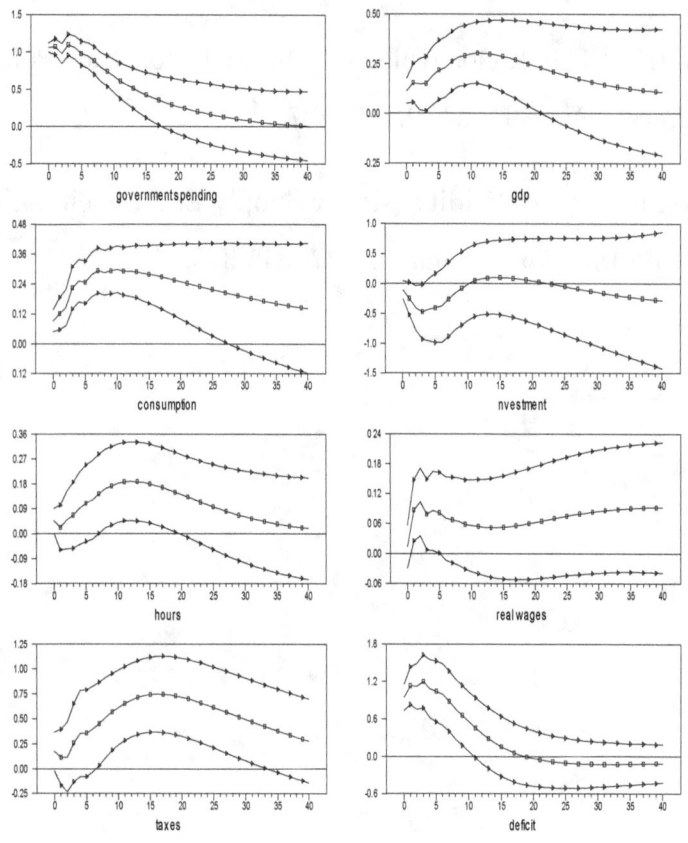

Figure 2. Determinacy Analysis

Baseline Calibration

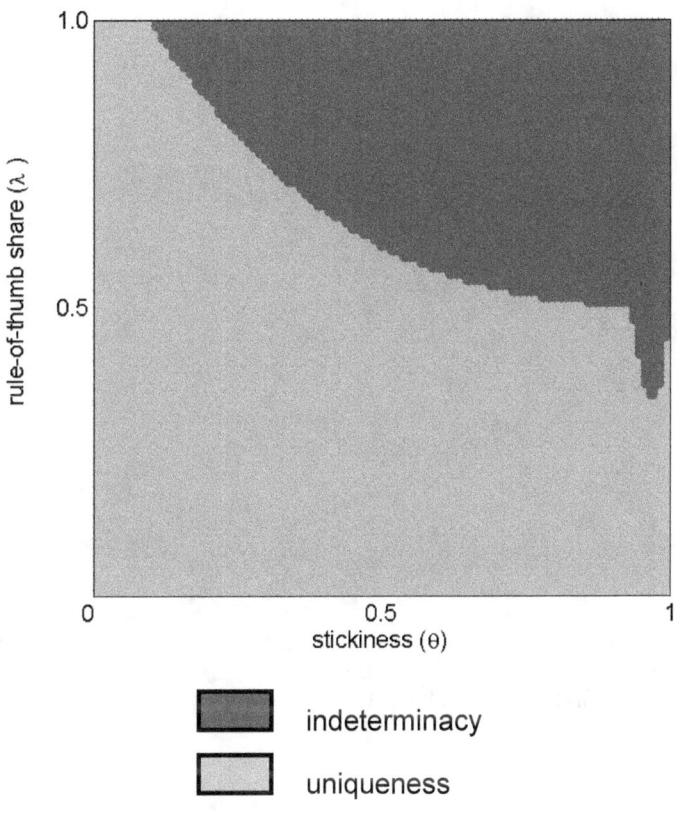

Figure 3. Impact Multipliers: Sensitivity to ρ_g

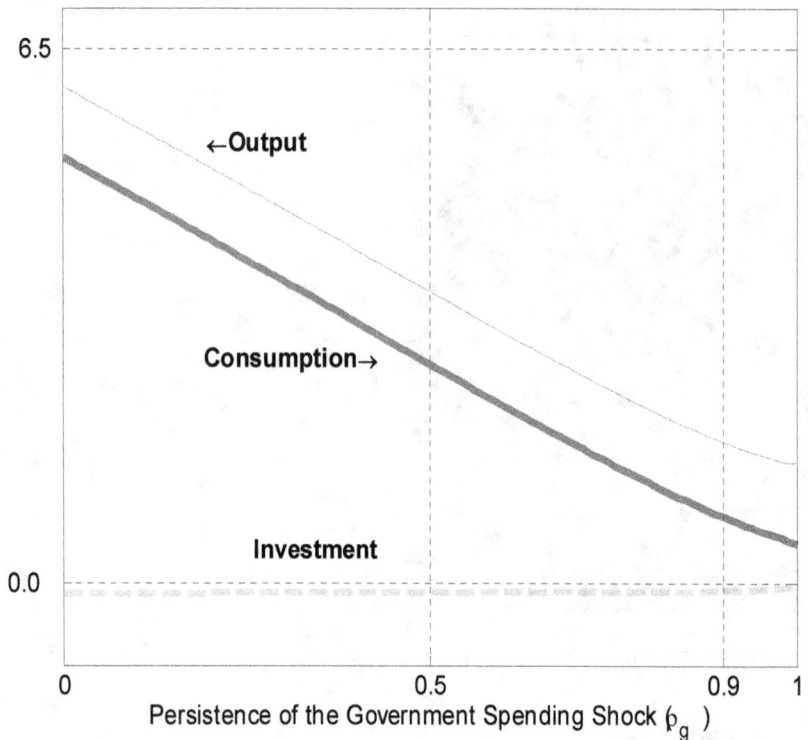

Figure 4. Impact Multipliers: Sensitivity to ρ_g

Alternative Calibrations

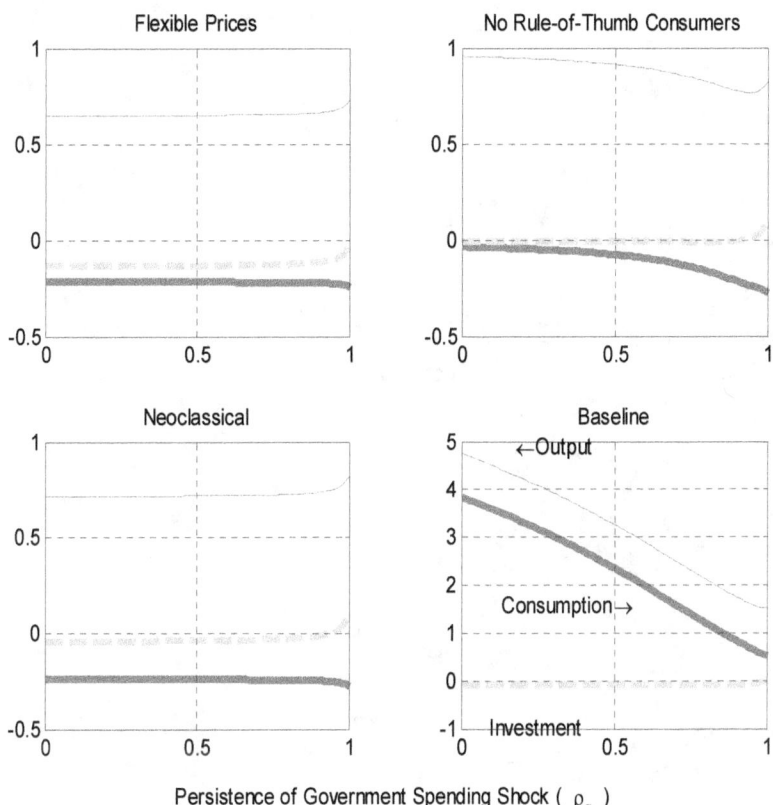

Persistence of Government Spending Shock (ρ_g)

Figure 5. Impulse Responses to a Government Spending Shock
Neoclassical vs. Baseline Models

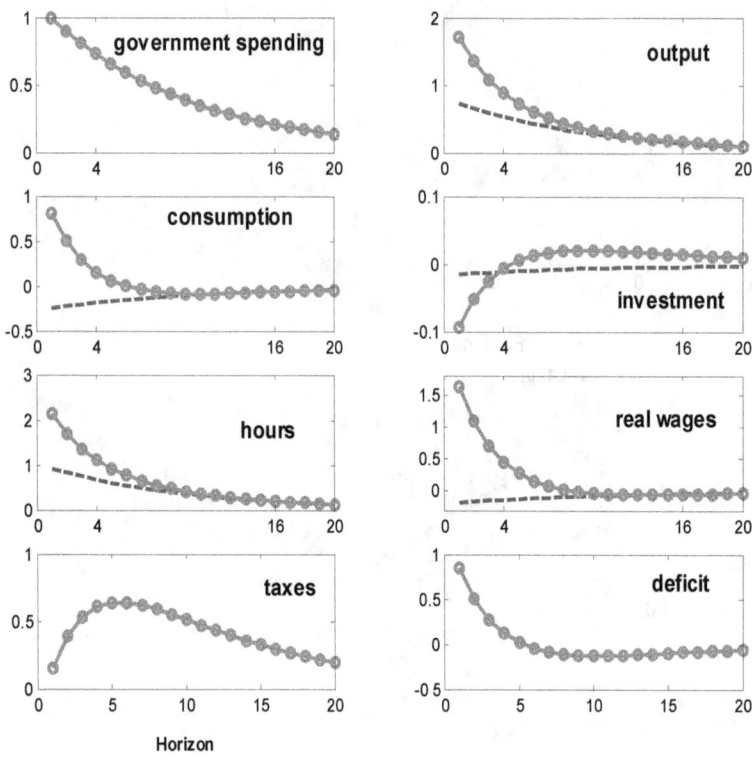

o-o-o **baseline model**
-------- **neoclassical model**

Figure 6. Impact Multipliers

Sensitivity to Non-Policy Parameters $\{\lambda, \theta, \eta, \psi\}$

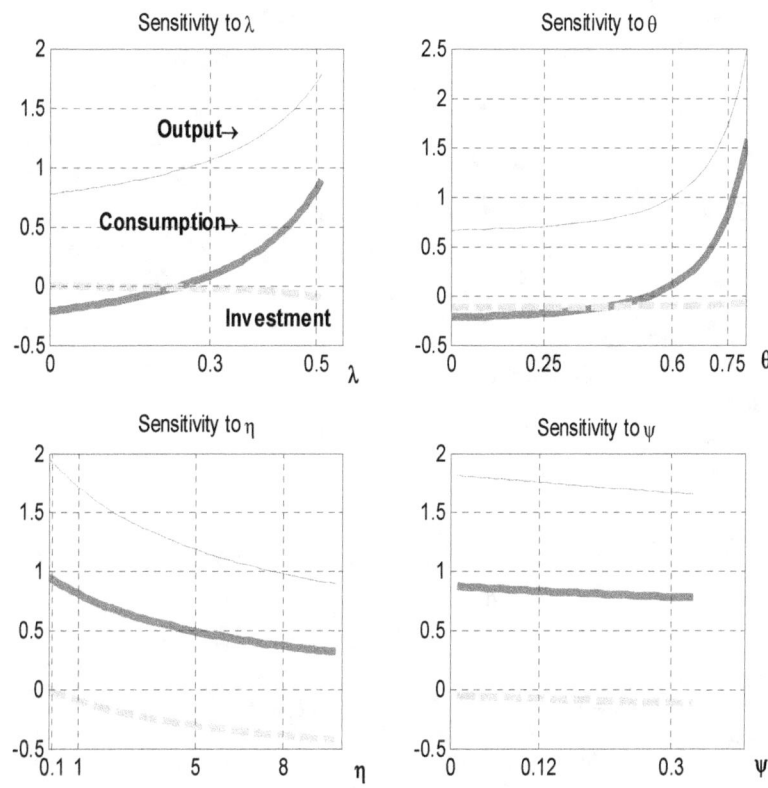

Figure 7. Impact Multipliers

Sensitivity to Policy Parameters $\{\phi_\pi, \phi_g, \phi_b\}$

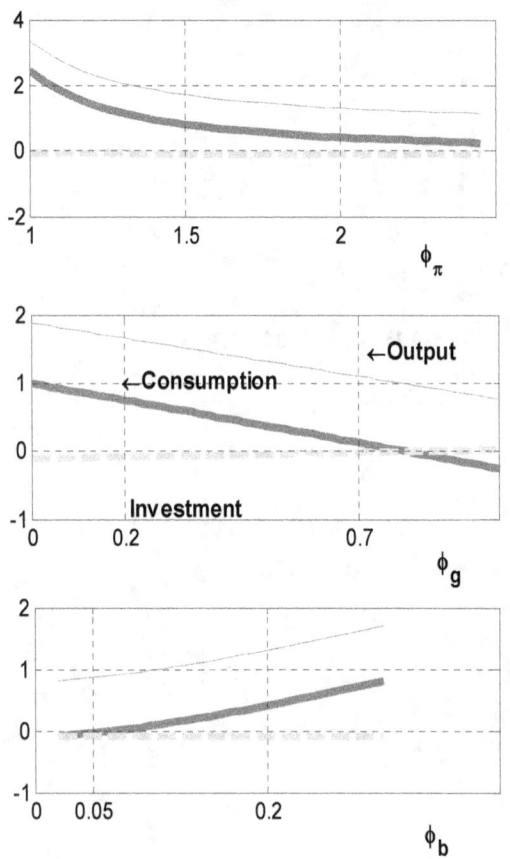